AUTO
RACING
HIGHLIGHTS

BY MARSHALL AND
SUE BURCHARD

GARRARD PUBLISHING COMPANY
CHAMPAIGN, ILLINOIS

Sports Consultant:
COLONEL RED REEDER
Former Member of the West Point Coaching Staff
and Special Assistant to the West Point
Director of Athletics

Photo Credits:

Automotive History Collection, Detroit Public Library: pp. 11 (both),
    33, 36 (center right and bottom), 39
Brown Brothers: pp. 4, 14, 23, 29, 36 (top and center left)
Culver Pictures: p. 52
Ford Archives, Henry Ford Museum, Dearborn, Michigan: p. 17
Indianapolis Motor Speedway: pp. 3, 49 (all), 60, 63, jacket
Long Island Automotive Museum, Southampton, New York: pp. 26, 42, 45
National Hot Rod Association: pp. 74, 76 (top)
Sports Car Club of America: p. 90 (all)
STP Corporation, Fort Lauderdale, Florida: p. 67 (bottom)
Wide World Photos: pp. 1, 66 (all), 67 (top and middle), 76 (bottom), 83 (all), 95

Library of Congress Cataloging in Publication Data

Burchard, Marshall.
    Auto racing highlights.

    SUMMARY: A brief history of auto racing in the
United States highlighting some of its famous partici-
pants and events.

    1. Automobile racing—United States—History—
Juvenile literature. [1. Automobile racing—History]
I. Burchard, Sue, joint author. II. Title.
GV1033.B77   796.7′2′0973   75-6692
ISBN 0-8116-6673-5

Contents

The cheering finish to an early automobile race in France.

1. FULL STEAM AHEAD!
The First Auto Race

Count Albert de Dion paced back and forth impatiently in front of his steam-driven automobile. From time to time he pulled out a large gold pocket watch and squinted at the dial. It was getting late!

The count stopped and watched closely as his mechanic shoveled hot coals into the firebox of the strange boxlike contraption on four wheels. The mechanic bent down and blew on the coals until they glowed. As the red-hot coals heated the water in the car's boiler, clouds of steam came pouring out.

"Is the car ready?" the count asked him.

"All set," said the mechanic. Then he placed a ladder against the car. The tall, elegantly dressed count climbed up the ladder to the high driver's seat. He took a firm grip on the steering stick, called the tiller.

The date was July 22, 1894. The place was Paris, France. The world's first automobile race was about to begin.

French inventors had been making cars since 1890, but most people saw little use for the new machines. So the men who made cars decided to hold a race. They wanted to prove that cars were the fastest way to travel long distances.

The race course was a dirt road that stretched for 78 miles between Paris and Rouen. The road was full of holes and ruts. None of the 21 racers, including the count, was sure that he could make it the whole way.

The clumsy cars moved to the starting line. Mechanics leaped aboard with their tools. When the cars were all lined up, the starter waved a flag, and the race began.

"Full steam ahead!" shouted the count.

Spectators covered their ears as the big cars roared and sputtered off down the road.

The count pulled into an early lead. Soon he was out of Paris and bumping along through the countryside. Above the roar of the engine, he heard some strange rattles. He gave his mechanic a worried look.

"You keep driving," the mechanic yelled. "I'll keep the car from falling apart!"

The drivers trying to catch the count soon faced a frightening problem. Flaming chunks of coal were flying out the back of his car. Many of the cars behind had gasoline engines. Sparks from the coals could easily set their gas tanks on fire. The drivers had to dodge a rain of sparks to keep from blowing up.

French farmers dropped their pitchforks and ran from their fields to see what the noise was all about. Many of them had never seen a car before. At first they stood with their mouths open and stared at the strange machines coming toward them. But they soon became angry when small fires started along the edge of the road. As they stamped out the fires, they shook their fists at the count.

"You fool!" they screamed. "Get that crazy thing off the road. You will set the world on fire!"

The count hardly noticed the angry shouts. Driving was so difficult that it was taking every bit of his attention. Each time his tires hit a rut, his car almost ran off the road. He had to pull on the tiller with all his strength to keep the heavy car from going into a ditch. While the count tried to steer, his mechanic climbed all over the bouncing car and tightened parts that shook loose.

After seven hours of driving, the count was the first to reach Rouen. His average speed was 11.9 miles per hour. No horse-drawn buggy could have traveled so fast for such a great distance.

The people who made cars were excited. The race had proved their point. Cars could be used to travel long distances. Almost at once the car makers made plans for an even longer race. The following year the French town-to-town race covered the unbelievable distance of 732 miles! The age of automobile racing had begun.

2. BEDFRAMES ON WHEELS
Racing Fever Comes to America

The first American car was built in 1893 by two brothers, Charles and Frank Duryea. This horseless carriage had a gasoline engine. It was smaller and lighter than the first European cars and had only one seat. A bicycle chain connected the engine to the rear wheels. A long stick, or tiller, was used for steering.

Other American inventors were working on cars at the same time. Soon they got together and planned America's first auto race.

The contest took place on Thanksgiving Day, November 28, 1895, between Chicago

This Duryea car, Number 5, won the historic race from Chicago to Evanston, Illinois held in 1895. The start of this race is shown below.

and Evanston, Illinois. The day was cold and windy. Snow covered the ground.

Six cars lined up for the start. Four of them, including the one driven by Frank Duryea, ran on gasoline. The others were powered by electricity.

In spite of the extreme cold, all the engines started. The six cars raced through the streets of downtown Chicago. Drivers had trouble making sharp turns and sometimes drove their cars right up on the sidewalks. Passersby jumped to get out of the way.

The cars soon left the city behind. They drove along the shore of Lake Michigan and headed for Evanston, 27 miles away. As they jolted along over the dirt road, the automobiles began to break down. Frank Duryea had to stop several times to make repairs. He also made stops to pick up cakes of ice to cool his engine.

When the cars reached Evanston, they turned around and headed back to the starting point in Chicago. Hundreds of people crowded around to cheer the victor. Only two drivers made it all the way. Frank Duryea arrived first. He was the winner of America's first automobile race with an average speed of 6.66 miles per hour. Since he had to stop so many times for repairs, it took him almost 24 hours to cover the 54-mile course.

As time went on, more and more American car races were run on short oval dirt tracks. Many of these were tracks used for horseracing at county or state fairs. The heavy racing machines scarred the dirt courses with ruts and holes, and both cars and drivers took a hard pounding.

The first car race to take place on an oval track was held at Narragansett Park, Rhode Island, on September 7, 1896. Seven

Two of the cars that took part in the
race at Narragansett Park.

cars took part in the race. Two cars were
electric powered. The other five, which
ran on gasoline, had been designed by
the Duryea brothers.

The cars went around and around the
track. Each complete turn around the
course was called a lap. The winner was
an electric car driven at an average
speed of 27 miles per hour.

Another important dirt-track race took
place in Grosse Pointe, Michigan. It was

14

held on October 25, 1902, and was called the Manufacturers Challenge Cup Race.

Everyone thought the fastest car entered was the Bullet, made by Cleveland auto maker Alexander Winton. For a whole year no car had been able to beat it. It could travel 50 miles per hour.

But three young men, whose names were Thomas Cooper, Henry Ford, and Harold Wills, were determined to beat the Bullet. Cooper, an ex-bicycle racer, put up the money. Ford, an ex-farmer and auto racer, designed the car. Wills, an engineer, built it and made it work.

Ford named the car after a famous train of the day, the 999. The big red car was a high-powered machine. The huge engine sat uncovered on the frame of the car. In back of the engine was a bucket seat for the driver, and in front of the seat was a steering stick. There was no body and no windshield.

The trouble with the 999 was that it roared like a freight train. And it was so heavy that no one could steer it. Driving it was very dangerous.

All three owners were afraid to drive the huge car. Finally Tom Cooper had an idea. He wired his friend Barney Oldfield and asked him if he'd like to try driving the 999. Oldfield was a trick bicycle racer. He had never driven a car in his life, but he wasn't afraid to take chances. He wired back an enthusiastic yes and took the first train to Detroit.

A few weeks before the Challenge Cup Race, the red monster arrived in Detroit by boat. From there a horse pulled the car to the track. The 999 could not be trusted on public roads.

Barney took one look at the car and laughed.

"It looks like a bedframe on wheels," he said.

Tom Cooper tried to drive the big car around the oval track, but he could not manage the steering.

"Let me try it now," Oldfield urged.

"This is no bicycle," Cooper warned. "This thing could kill you."

Because he had such powerful arms, Barney Oldfield was able to control the steering stick and hold the car on the track. It was decided that Oldfield should drive the 999 in the race.

Barney Oldfield at the steering stick of the 999. Henry Ford stands proudly by.

Oldfield practiced driving the huge car every day. Soon he was handling the 999 as easily as his bicycle.

When the race started Oldfield surprised the crowd by taking a big lead at once. The Bullet was not even close.

Oldfield drove like crazy. He went around curves as fast as he drove on the straight part of the track. The Bullet fell farther and farther behind. Oldfield drove the 999 to an easy victory.

Oldfield's win made people aware of Henry Ford's car designs. Soon after the race, Ford was able to raise enough money to start the Ford Motor Company. The Challenge Cup Race was important enough to start Henry Ford on his career as the man who put America on wheels.

Ford and Cooper soon broke up their partnership, but Wills became an important figure in the Ford Motor Company.

And daring Barney Oldfield became the

most famous and most colorful racing driver in the nation. He put together a traveling racing show that performed at county fairs all around the United States.

The drivers wore wild costumes. Often they dressed as "good guys" and "bad guys." The crowds cheered for the heroes. They booed and hissed the villains.

Barney Oldfield would do almost anything to please the crowds that came to his shows. He crashed through fences. He often was trapped in wrecked cars.

In one race he chipped all of his front teeth. After that he always raced with a cigar clamped between his teeth. He said he used the cigar as a cushion for his teeth when he went over bad bumps.

Barney's fans loved his wild, circus-style of racing, but some people thought his antics gave racing a bad name. They wanted to start a more serious kind of automobile racing in the United States.

3. ELECTRIC, STEAM, AND GASOLINE
The Vanderbilt Cup Races

One of the people who wanted to see the sport of auto racing become more respectable was William K. Vanderbilt, Jr., a very rich American from Long Island. From the time automobiles were first invented, Vanderbilt had been interested in them. He was interested in automobile races too.

The early auto makers—men like the Duryea brothers, Henry Ford, Ransom Eli Olds, Alexander Winton, and the Studebaker brothers—were interested in auto racing too. They tried different kinds of power to make their cars go.

20

There were cars powered by electricity, some by steam, and others by gasoline. Most car makers finally decided to use gasoline because gasoline-powered cars went faster and did not break down so often.

In the space of a few years, the automobile was a greatly improved machine. People no longer thought of it as a useless toy. Soon after 1900 there were many cars chugging along the public roads of America. Many proud car owners wanted to see their cars in a race.

Mr. Vanderbilt decided to hold a race in which the best cars and drivers from Europe and America could compete against each other. He felt the time was right for America's first serious road race.

Invitations were sent to American and European car makers who might want to take part in the first Vanderbilt Cup Race in October 1904. Vanderbilt ordered a cup three feet tall to be given as a prize to the winner. It was made of 40 pounds of solid silver. Car makers from France, Germany, Italy, and the United States accepted Vanderbilt's invitation.

Mr. Vanderbilt wanted the race to test the skill and daring of the drivers as well as the strength and speed of the cars.

A course was laid out on public roads in the center of Long Island. The course was 28 miles long and shaped like a triangle. The drivers had to drive around it ten times.

The route was difficult. It ran through farmland, and only part of it was paved. The roads were so narrow in places that it was hard for cars to pass one another. Railroad and trolley tracks crossed the route at five points. At each crossing drivers would have to slow down to 10 miles per hour. They would have to go

William K. Vanderbilt, Jr. (left), sponsor
of the nation's "first serious road race."

even slower when they drove through
one of the towns on the route. Men on
bicycles pedaled ahead of the cars to
warn people to get out of the way.

The farmers in the area were told to
keep off the roads and to keep their
animals and children out of the way.

Some of the farmers said they would
get out their guns and shoot the racing
cars off the road. Fortunately, they didn't
carry out their threats, and the race took
place as planned.

Thousands of people came from New York City to watch the race. They stood at the start and finish lines and along the sides of the roads.

On the morning of the race, the drivers began to warm up their cars before the sun rose. Long flames leaping out of the exhausts lit up the darkness. The air was filled with the smell of gasoline.

Eighteen powerful cars gathered around the starting line with their engines roaring. It was still dark when the starter waved his green flag and shouted "Go!" to the first driver. Every two minutes he waved his flag to send another driver on his way. Soon all the cars were speeding along the country roads. The dust pouring out behind the fast-moving machines made it hard to see. Stones shot up from beneath the spinning wheels as the drivers pressed their gas pedals to the floor.

Early in the race, cars started running into trouble. The driver of a French Renault dropped out when his motor sputtered and died after making only one lap around the course. The driver of an Italian Fiat quit after his clutch wore out.

The tires on all the cars became dangerously hot. The drivers stopped every few miles to spray their wheels with cold water. Many tires blew out anyway. A punctured tire from a German Mercedes flew from its wheel. The bare rim of the wheel got caught in a trolley car track and flipped the Mercedes over. The driver was not hurt badly, but the mechanic was killed.

Another Mercedes had an accident too. When the driver stopped for repairs, the mechanic crawled under the car to see what was wrong. By mistake the driver stepped on the gas and ran over the

George Heath, the first Vanderbilt Cup winner, at the starting line.

mechanic. The mechanic was badly injured, but he lived.

One of the American Pope-Toledos was going so fast that its steering system broke. The car flew off the road and ran full speed into a tree. The car was a total wreck. But the driver and the mechanic escaped with no more than a bad shaking up and a few scratches.

Most of the spectators had never before seen such a race. They got so excited that they stood in the middle of the road and waited for the racers to come by. At the last possible moment, they dashed to the side and let the speeding cars pass. The biggest problem the drivers had was trying not to run into the enthusiastic racing fans.

Finally, after 6 hours and 56 minutes, the winning car crossed the finish line. It was a French Panhard driven by George Heath, an American. His average speed for the 280-mile course was 52 miles per hour. Another French car finished second. An American car, a Pope-Toledo driven by Herbert Lytle, would have been third. But, as Lytle was nearing the finish line, the spectators got carried away with excitement. They ran yelling out onto the roadway. The officials feared for the lives of the cheering mob and called the race to a halt.

Mr. Vanderbilt was happy with the performance of the American cars and drivers. He thought the race was a smashing success. He decided to hold the event every fall.

Each year more and more people came to the Vanderbilt Cup Race. In 1906 spectators began to arrive at the race course a day ahead of time. All night long they came. By morning, when the race was supposed to begin, there were 250,000 people standing along the route.

The start was delayed for fifteen minutes because a thick fog hung over part of the course. When the fog lifted, the cars sped away from the starting line in a cloud of dust. The race was on.

The eager crowd pushed forward to get a better view. A thousand policemen tried to push the crowd back. Traveling at speeds of more than 70 miles per hour, drivers panicked at the sight of the milling people.

Crowds lined the route of the Vanderbilt Cup Race and spilled over into the road.

One driver stopped and yelled to a track official, "If you cannot control this crowd, there is sure to be a disaster!"

Mr. Vanderbilt drove along the road in his white Mercedes. He begged the onlookers to stay out of the path of the cars, but it was no use. The most powerful car in the race, a Hotchkiss, hit a man who was standing in the middle of the road. The man was killed instantly. Two boys were run over by other cars and badly hurt.

The *New York Times* called the race "a terrible slaughter." Since there did not seem to be any way to control the crowds lining public roads, Mr. Vanderbilt said that there would be no race the following year. The Vanderbilt Cup races were held again, beginning in 1908, but the crowds were still uncontrollable. After the 1916 race, Mr. Vanderbilt sadly called off the races for good.

4. NEW YORK TO PARIS
The Incredible Around-the-World Race

It was a bitter cold day in February 1908. Six open cars with folding canvas tops were lined up in Times Square in New York City. They were ready to leave on the first leg of a race from New York to Paris, France. The drivers huddled into their furs and warm overcoats and stamped their feet to keep warm. A crowd of 250,000 people was on hand to give the drivers a send-off.

The *New York Times*, a French newspaper, and a Chicago newspaper were the sponsors of the 17,000-mile race, the longest ever held.

The cars would drive west across the United States. They would then travel by boat from Seattle, Washington, to Alaska. From there they would drive across the frozen waters of the Bering Strait to Russia and continue by land to Paris. It would be a fantastic test for men and machines.

There had been many improvements in the motor car since its invention in the 1880s, but it was not yet dependable. A motor could quit at any time. Because there were few gas and service stations, a driver had to carry a repair kit and spare parts and know how to fix his own car.

Tires were still a big problem. The first tires were made out of iron. Later they were solid rubber. Air-filled rubber tires came next, but they were so weak that a sharp stone could poke a hole in them.

The Zust and the Protos line up in Times
Square to start the around-the-world race.

Changing a tire was almost enough to
break a driver's back. If the ground was
soft, it was difficult to jack up the car
to work on it. The whole tire had to be
pried off the wheel, and a new inner
tube had to be put inside. After that
the poor, tired driver had to put the
tire back on the wheel and pump it up
with a small hand pump. Pumping air
into a tire took from 10 to 20 minutes.

Roads were another problem. In cities

and towns the roads were fairly good, but in the country roads were terrible. The dirt roads were rutted and littered with rocks. Often they stopped suddenly.

In dry weather clouds of dust made it hard for drivers to see and breathe. In wet weather a heavy car would sink deep into the soft mud. A driver sometimes had to walk for miles to find a farmer and borrow a horse to pull his auto out of the mud.

In spite of these problems, there were drivers who were eager to take part in the around-the-world race. The United States, Germany, and Italy each entered one car. France entered three cars.

The American entry was a Thomas Flyer. It had an open top and a 40-horsepower engine. Thick wooden planks were fastened like shelves to both sides of the car. These could be removed and used as tracks through mud and snow.

Large boxes tied to the running boards were filled with tools, spare parts, and food for the driving team of two men. The car also carried fuel, oil lanterns, and a strong rope. Four spare tires were lashed to the back. An American flag stuck up from the spare tires.

The French carried some even stranger items. They brought a set of skis to hitch on in areas of deep snow. They also had a set of wheels covered with steel studs to use for winter driving. These were the first snow tires.

The French had one more unusual piece of equipment: a mast and sail. They planned to unfurl the sail in wide open country where the wind was blowing. It would save on fuel.

At 11:15 A. M. the starter fired a shot from a small gold gun to send the six cars on their way. The crowd cheered wildly as the cars started with a roar

And not a snowplow in sight! The drivers slog through heavy snow, ride on the tracks, brave the cold, and dig out after a blizzard.

and rolled north on Broadway. The cars were headed for Albany, New York, the goal for the first day's drive.

It wasn't long before the racers ran into trouble. Soon after leaving New York City, they drove into a blinding snowstorm. Again and again they had to stop and shovel a path through snowdrifts.

The snow was hard on men and machines. One of the French cars slid into a snowdrift and broke its rear axle. It had to drop out of the race.

Montague Roberts and George Schuster, the American drivers, had problems too. Pushing through the heavy snow proved too much for the engine, and one of the cylinders broke down. The team had to stop for repairs.

Progress was slow. By the time the cars reached Iowa and Nebraska, it was almost spring. The snow had melted and turned the roads into rivers of mud. The cars sank in up to their hubcaps. The crews had to climb out into the sticky mud and push. Often it took a team of horses to pull an auto free.

A second French team had to give up. Covered from head to toe with mud, they were much too discouraged to go on. Now there were only four cars left in the race.

The cars were far apart as they drove across the western plains. Here rough wagon and horse trails were the main travel routes. Roberts and Schuster decided they would make better time if they used the Union Pacific Railroad tracks. They pushed their heavy car up onto the track. It made the going easier, but it was no speedway. Bumping over the wooden ties was hard on tires. They kept blowing out and had to be changed. Each time a train came along, the team had to lift the car off the tracks and then put it on again after the train had passed.

At Cheyenne, Wyoming, Roberts decided that he had had enough. An eager young man named Linn Matthewson took over for him.

Crew and bystanders drag the Thomas Flyer out of a mudhole in Colorado.

More dangers had to be faced when the cars reached the Rocky Mountains. The cars bumped along narrow mountain trails. The Italian team almost drove off a cliff. Their front wheels were hanging in space. The team had to step very carefully out of their car to keep it from crashing down the mountainside. Luckily, they were able to push it back onto solid ground and continue on their way.

Leaving the Rocky Mountains behind, Schuster and Matthewson were delighted to find the Thomas Flyer far in the lead. They drove through the wind-swept deserts of Nevada and on into California. They finally rolled into San Francisco on March 24. They had crossed the United States, a distance of 3,836 miles, in 42 days.

At this point, the Italians were still struggling through the rugged country in Utah. They were in second place. But the French and German teams were even farther behind, in Wyoming.

The Americans made much needed repairs. Then they drove on to Seattle, Washington, where they boarded a ship for Alaska.

The American team landed at Valdez, Alaska, on April 8. The racers took one look at the area and saw that driving there would be impossible. The streets were seas of mud. There would be no way to get through the country beyond. They sent telegrams to New York City telling racing officials of their plight.

The officials met and decided to change the course of the race. They told the American team to return to Seattle and take a ship to Yokohama, Japan. The new route would take them across Japan first and then, by ship, to Vladivostok, Russia.

The American drivers were angry and

disappointed when they got back to Seattle eight days later. The French and Italian teams were already on their way across the Pacific. The German car had broken down in Utah and had been carried by freight train to San Francisco.

Schuster and Matthewson complained bitterly. Racing officials decided to penalize the Germans for carrying their car on a train by adding fifteen days to their driving time. To make up for the time lost in going to Alaska, they took away fifteen days from the Americans' time.

The German team left Seattle on April 19; the Americans left two days later.

Carts and cars alike sank into the Siberian mud.

The long sea voyage gave both teams a chance to rest. When the Americans reached Yokohama, they learned that the German team had sailed directly to Vladivostok. Racing officials penalized the Germans by adding fifteen more days to their driving time.

When all of the teams assembled in Vladivostok, they were surprised to hear that the French were dropping out of the race. It was spring as the remaining cars started across Russia. The rivers were full from heavy rains and melting snow. Everywhere there were floods. One river overflowed its banks and trapped the Italian car. The crew had to abandon it and swim to higher ground and safety. The Italians were able to rescue their car later. But it took so many days to dry out the engine that they got hopelessly behind in the race.

The American and German teams had

problems with floods, too, and in some places it was still cold and snowy. The trip across Russia seemed endless. Often the crews slept in their open cars, and snow almost buried them in their seats. Their faces and fingers were frostbitten.

The American and German teams battled for first place as they continued west across the vast Russian countryside. First one, then the other took the lead. By the time they reached Germany, the German team was well ahead.

The Germans got to Paris on July 26. Schuster and Matthewson arrived four days later on the evening of July 30. Because of the penalty for carrying their car on a train and skipping the Japanese portion of the trip, the German team had to settle for second place. The American Flyer was declared the winner.

Thousands of Frenchmen turned out to cheer the tired and dirty travelers. The

The Flyer returns in triumph to New York.

Americans had driven a grueling 13,341 miles in five months and two weeks. The Italian team chugged into Paris a month and a half after the Americans.

It was a great victory for American auto makers. They had proved without a doubt that an American car was as good as any European car.

The contest was intended to be a test for automobiles. It also showed the incredible strength, courage, and determination of the men who drove them.

5. A CARNIVAL OF SPEED

The Opening of Indianapolis Speedway

In the years before World War I, automobile racing in Europe and the United States went in two different directions. European sports fans liked Grand Prix road racing best. Americans seemed to prefer the sight of fast cars racing on closed tracks.

American racing drivers traveled from one track to another. Since the prize money was usually small, the drivers raced mostly for thrills. Barney Oldfield, Eddie Rickenbacker, and Ralph DePalma were some of the most popular pioneer drivers.

46

At this time most of the American tracks were small and dirt surfaced. Carl Fisher, an Indiana businessman, decided that the United States needed a first-rate big track. In 1909 Fisher and three rich friends bought over 328 acres of land just west of the city of Indianapolis, Indiana. On it they built the biggest closed track in the nation. The 2.5-mile track was in the shape of a huge oval. There was a banked turn at each corner. Fisher wanted to pave the track with bricks, but he and his partners decided that brick was too costly. Instead, the track was covered with a layer of crushed limestone and gravel.

The four men built the Indianapolis Speedway mainly for auto racing. They wanted to attract the best drivers in the nation to put on the most exciting races held anywhere. These men also wanted to give car makers a place to test new mechanical features for racing cars as well as for cars in general use. They hoped that the Speedway would serve as a testing ground to make automobiles stronger.

The Indianapolis Speedway opened for auto racing on Thursday, August 19, 1909. Three days of competition were planned. Ads called it "A Carnival of Speed." Barney Oldfield, constantly chewing a big black cigar, mingled with the happy crowds and shared their picnic lunches before the races began.

In one of the first day's events, the cars were supposed to circle the track 100 times for a total distance of 250 miles. As they whizzed around the gravel track, their tires kicked up huge swirls of dust. The dust clouds made it difficult for drivers to see. In one crash both the driver and his mechanic were killed.

In a one-mile race on Friday, Barney

The race is on! The starting line of one
of the first-day races at Indy, August 19,
1909 (top); a typical pit stop (middle); the
ten-mile free-for-all underway (bottom).

Oldfield drove a powerful Mercedes as recklessly as ever. He set a new world's record, winning at an average speed of 83.51 miles per hour. Barney had a close call in Friday's ten-mile event when his engine caught on fire. The hood of the car blew off, but Barney managed to duck. Luckily there were no other accidents on Friday.

The events came to an end with a 300-mile race on Saturday. On the first lap the cars stirred up dust clouds so thick that drivers were completely blinded. Soon a car crashed through a fence. The driver lived, but his mechanic and two spectators were killed. Worried officials stopped the race and told the crowd to go home.

Carl Fisher and his friends had two choices. They could close the track, or they could pave it to make it safer. They decided to pave it. It took workmen 63 days to lay down 3,200,000 paving bricks at a cost of $155,000. The new nickname for the Indianapolis Speedway was the Brickyard.

Indianapolis held a 500-mile race on Memorial Day, May 30, 1911. More than 80,000 people came to watch.

The 500-mile Indianapolis speed contest has become a national event and one of the most important racing competitions in the world.

In the first Indy 500, a little-known driver named Ray Harroun caused a problem for the officials. He wanted to drive without a mechanic.

"You can't do that," argued one official. "It won't be safe. You will need a man to watch out for cars coming up behind you."

"OK," said Harroun. "I'll put a mirror on my car. That way I'll be able to see what's in back."

The officials finally agreed. Harroun bolted a mirror onto the body of his Marmon Wasp. It was the first rear-view mirror ever used on an automobile.

Forty cars started. The loud noise of their engines was almost deafening. For a long time no one paid much attention to Ray Harroun. He was almost in last place.

Toward the middle of the race, many of the cars began to have problems. Several racers blew tires. Others had engine trouble.

Ray Harroun and his Marmon Wasp won the first Indy 500 handily. Notice his rear-view mirror.

Ray Harroun knew more about cars than most of the other drivers. During the practice runs before the race, he had carefully figured out how fast he could drive to get the best wear out of his tires. After trying out several speeds, he discovered that his tires would last the longest if he drove at 75 miles per hour.

As cars passed him by, Ray Harroun kept his Marmon Wasp at a steady speed of 75 miles per hour. He could have driven a little faster, but he was counting on outlasting the other cars.

His plan worked. As more cars dropped out, Harroun gradually moved up to the front. He was in second place with only a few laps to go when the last remaining automobile in front of him broke down. He took the lead and held it. Cautious driving and knowing a lot about tires made Ray Harroun the first man to win the Indianapolis 500.

6. THE MILLION DOLLAR RACE
The Memorial Day Classic at Indy

The Indy 500 quickly became the most famous automobile race in the United States. It has had a long and interesting history.

European drivers competed in the 500 for the first time in 1913. A French driver, Jules Goux, won that year in a Peugeot. The race the following year was also won by a Frenchman.

In 1915, for the first time, the starting positions were decided by trial runs before the big race. Before the 500 began, each car was timed with a stopwatch as it made a number of runs around the track. The car with the fastest average time was given the best starting position. A good starting position had a lot to do with who won the race.

By 1917 the United States had been drawn into World War I. Indianapolis Speedway closed down and was turned into a place to repair airplanes. The track itself was used as a landing strip. After the war the races began again. But only cars designed especially for racing were allowed to compete.

Over the years the makers of cars for general use had been losing interest in entering their cars in races. Gradually the sport came to be dominated by pure racers—cars designed to get top speed under race track conditions. One of these engineers was Harry Miller, who would become the top racing car designer in America. The streamlined Miller racers were put together just as carefully as watches. For a while they were almost unbeatable.

Fred and Augie Duesenberg, who were brothers, began making cars to compete with the Miller racers. The Duesenberg brothers were also careful craftsmen, and their cars won many times at Indianapolis.

The Miller and Duesenberg racing cars were as fast and as beautiful as any in the world. But they were also expensive. They cost about $25,000 each.

In 1927 Eddie Rickenbacker bought the Indianapolis Speedway from the owners. Rickenbacker had been a very popular racing driver before World War I. During the war he flew in over a hundred air battles and became an American hero. But he never lost his love of auto racing.

Rickenbacker made some changes in the Speedway that he thought would make the track more popular. He built a golf course in the middle of it. He changed the rules for cars to encourage companies that made autos for general use to enter the race again. One rule said that pure racing machines, like the Millers and the Duesenbergs, had to have smaller and less powerful engines. Rickenbacker's plan worked. Buick, Chrysler, Ford, Hudson, Packard, and Studebaker began to take part. They turned some of their standard cars into racers. But the pure racing machines still won most of the time.

The biggest winner during the 1930s was an excitable little man named Wilbur Shaw. He drove in every Indy 500 between 1927 and 1941. He was one of the few drivers to win the Indy three times. But it took Shaw ten tries before he won his first race.

During the 1931 time trials, Shaw's car broke down and could not be fixed in time for the race. Shaw was very disappointed. Then Fred Duesenberg walked over and asked Wilbur if he would drive one of the gleaming white Duesenbergs entered in the race. Shaw was delighted. It was the chance of a lifetime. The fact that he had never driven one of the huge, powerful Duesenbergs did not matter to him.

Shaw was a small man. The car had been built for a much taller driver. When Wilbur crawled into the cockpit, he had to sit forward in the seat to be able to reach the gas pedal. He had to lean his head out the side in order to see.

With a quick nod to Otto Hannowsky, the mechanic who rode with him, Wilbur jerked the car into gear. The Duesenberg rumbled out onto the track.

Shaw was not used to driving such a heavy car. He thought he was moving along too slowly.

"Is this big brute in high gear?" he screamed to the mechanic.

Otto nodded happily. Soon they passed a few cars.

"Do I have the throttle wide open?" Shaw shouted.

Again, Otto nodded.

Wilbur was unhappy. He was sure he was not making good time. Actually he was doing very well. He was surprised when suddenly he found himself in fifth place.

Wilbur was approaching the straight part of the track. In his usual daring manner, he decided to pass all the cars ahead of him at one time. He pressed down hard on the gas pedal and swung out. He passed three cars successfully, but, when he tried to overtake the last remaining one, the long straightaway was nearly used up. The hard wall of the third turn loomed ahead.

The leading car would not move over. Wilbur's tires lost their grip on the road

Wilbur Shaw's Duesenberg leaps over
the wall in a dramatic close call.

in the turn. The Duesenberg shot into
the air, soared over the wall, and van-
ished from sight. The other drivers were
sure they would never see Wilbur again.

An ambulance rushed Wilbur and his
mechanic to the Speedway hospital. They
were only slightly injured. Doctors ban-
daged his bruises, and then Shaw hurried
back to the pits. He thought that Fred
Duesenberg would be very angry at him
for destroying the expensive racing car.

60

Instead, the car designer, after making sure that Wilbur was all right, asked him to drive the other Duesenberg he had entered in the race. He called in the long white car, and the driver jumped out. Again Wilbur leaped into the too big cockpit and wriggled forward until he could reach the gas pedal. Leaning out so he could see, he roared back into action.

Once again he closed in on the leaders. The leading drivers glanced back and did a doubletake. They thought they were seeing a ghost.

Wilbur did not win the race, but his flying leap over the wall became a colorful part of Indy 500 history.

The Speedway stood silent and empty during World War II. In 1946 racing began again, but it did not really hit its stride until the 1950s.

If Wilbur Shaw was the most outstanding

driver of the 1930s, it was Bill Vukovich who was the best-known driver during the early 1950s. His nickname was Vukie, but he was better known to racing fans as the Mad Russian. He was quiet and liked to be alone. He had no fear of the high-speed oval. When young drivers asked him for advice, Vukie said, "You just step on the throttle and turn left."

Vukovich was a hot rookie in 1951. He easily took the lead in the 1952 Indy and held onto it. But just when he was about to cross the finish line, his steering broke down. The second place driver, Troy Ruttman, flashed by to win.

Vukie exploded with rage, "Ruttman never won an easier one, but you can be sure I won't let it happen again next year!"

The 1953 Indy took place on a boiling hot day. Driver after driver dropped out because of the extreme heat. Each time he came into the pits, Vukie poured two paper cups of cold water on the back of his neck. Then he charged back out onto the track. He wanted to win and win big. He did. When he crossed the finish line in first place, the next driver was eight miles behind.

Vukovich won again in 1954. With two wins in a row, he was determined to take the next as well. No one had ever

Vukovich's second trip to Victory Lane in 1954.

won three in a row. The 1955 race turned into a fight for the lead between Vukie and a driver named Jack McGrath. For the first hundred miles, they took turns leading. Then tragedy struck. Two cars in front of Vukovich ran into each other. One of them, driven by Johnny Boyd, was knocked into the path of Vukie's car. Vukovich ran full speed over the wheel of Boyd's car and flew into the air. His car cleared the wall without touching it. It did a complete turn in the air and landed nose first. Bill Vukovich died when his car hit the ground.

The skill and daring of great drivers like Bill Vukovich have always brought fans to the races. But another important purpose of the Indianapolis Speedway has been to serve as a proving ground for new ideas in car building. One such new idea was the turbine-powered car. In 1967 Andy Granatelli and his company entered a turbocar in the Indy 500. It was powered by a jet rather than an ordinary piston-type engine and ran on kerosine rather than on ordinary fuel. The turbocar didn't roar as race cars are supposed to do. Instead it whizzed by with hardly a sound.

Other car owners and drivers were angry and protested against the powerful turbocar. They said the machine was more like an airplane on wheels than a car. They thought they didn't stand a chance against it.

The turbine-powered car was driven by Parnelli Jones. He scooted into the lead with such ease that the crowd was stunned. When there were only five laps to go, Jones suddenly glided to a stop. A. J. Foyt charged into the lead and won the race. A six dollar gearbox in the turbine had broken and brought the million dollar car to a halt.

The Indy 500, a national institution! Fans pack the stands (above left); Gordon Johncock races to victory in 1973 (left); A. J. Foyt and Johnny Rutherford compete for first in 1974 (below).

A quick pit stop by A. J. Foyt is completed in only eighteen seconds (above); Bobby Unser (6) leads the pack to the starting line in 1972 (right); the turbocar that almost won the race in 1967 (below).

There were so many complaints against the jet engines that the following year racing officials told Granatelli that he could not use his powerful turbocar on the Indy track. Unhappily, he went back to using standard racing engines in his cars.

Today's Indy car is a strange, lopsided beast. Since all the turns on the Indy track are made to the left, the engine is on the left side of the car. The transmission is also on the left. Placing most of the weight on this side of the car makes left turns at high speed easier. A car in the Indy 500 circles the track counterclockwise 200 times, making four left turns on each lap. If an Indy car tried a right turn at racing speed, it would roll over.

A 50-gallon tank holds enough fuel to take the car a little over 125 miles. The tank is refilled three times during the race. The car rolls into the pit, and mechanics get to work at once. One man sticks an air hose into the side of the car. Four legs spring down from its body, and the car flies off the ground. Men attack all four wheels at once. A few taps knock off the hubcaps. A few more taps knock on the new wheels. At the same time fuel is forced into the tank by a powerful pump. When the car rolls on the track again, barely 23 seconds will have passed, and the car will have taken on 50 gallons of fuel and had all four tires changed.

It takes today's Indy drivers about three and one-half hours to complete the 200 laps. They get up to the dangerous speed of over 200 miles per hour on the straightaways. But to the drivers, the race is worth the risk. Over $1,000,000 in prize money is divided among the winners. No other race in the world offers more fame or money than the Indy 500.

7. HOT RODS AND RAILS
The Drag Racers

A new kind of auto racing became popular in the United States after World War II. It was called drag racing.

During the war no auto races had been held. Most of the drivers and mechanics were away fighting. Gasoline and rubber were too valuable to waste on sport.

The automobile factories stopped making cars. Instead they built tanks, trucks, and airplane engines. By the time the war ended in 1945, most cars on the road were almost worn out. Americans could hardly wait to go out and buy new ones.

The nation's auto makers began turning

out more cars than ever before. The new cars were faster than ever before too. Their big eight-cylinder engines could move them at speeds of 90 miles an hour. Soon more than a million of the fast new cars were rushing along the roadways of America.

There were many drivers now, especially teen-agers, who could not resist the urge to race the car next to them on a highway. Often two young drivers would pull up next to each other at a stoplight.

"Do you want to drag race?" one would shout.

"Sure," the other would answer.

The instant the light changed, they would both let out the clutch and slam the gas pedal all the way to the floor. Side by side the cars would screech off down the road. The object of this was to see who could get off to the fastest start.

Teen-agers who knew something about engines began to tinker with their cars to make them still more powerful. They made them so fast that people called the cars hot rods.

The roar of engines and the screech of tires disturbed the calm of neighborhoods at all hours of the day and night. People were disturbed by the noise and upset because hot-rodding was dangerous. Too many young people were being killed or injured in crashes.

In the 1950s Americans demanded that the police put a stop to hot-rodding. Boys caught drag racing were arrested. Sometimes their driver's licenses were taken away from them.

The hot-rodders refused to quit. Instead they started holding their drag races on quiet stretches of highway far from town. They posted lookouts at each end of the course to keep watch for the police.

When the police came hot-rodders would scatter.

Parents were worried because bad accidents were taking place at the secret drag strips. They decided they could prevent injuries by making drag races legal. They helped the teen-agers form hot-rod clubs. They arranged to block off parts of airfields and highways for races. They made the young drivers follow strict safety rules. All the cars had to have a strong metal bar, called a roll bar, built in over the driver's seat. The roll bar protected the driver if the car turned over. Drivers were required to wear helmets.

Since then, drag racing has become one of America's fastest growing sports.

The cars are divided into classes so that vehicles of the same weight and engine power compete against each other. There are so many different kinds of

The Christmas Tree flashes green, and
a pair of funny cars blasts off.

cars that they have been divided into
more than 100 different classes. Two cars
run at a time. The distance covered is
usually one quarter of a mile.

Most of the drivers are amateurs who
race for the fun of it. Their automobiles,
like the original hot rods, are ordinary
passenger cars that have been "souped
up" to make them faster.

Professional drivers race several different kinds of cars. Two of the most
popular ones are funny cars and dragsters.

74

Funny cars are plastic or fiberglass replicas of passenger cars. They have custom-built chassis and engines that allow them to race at fantastic speeds.

Dragsters look like no other cars on earth. In many of these machines the driver sits right behind the rear wheels. Two huge treadless tires, known as "slicks," almost hide him from view. A mighty 1,500-horsepower engine sits directly in front of him, practically in his lap. Long, low-slung sections of thin metal tubes reach forward to connect with a pair of small front wheels. Because of the tubes these special cars are known as "rails."

When two rails race, it is on pavement about the width of a four-lane highway and one-quarter mile long. The drivers move up to the starting line and watch the seven flashing lights on a tall pole nicknamed the Christmas Tree. While the yellow lights blink on and off five times,

These dragsters (top) are hurtling along at speeds of more than 200 miles per hour. Below, a driver opens his parachute to help stop his dragster.

the drivers gun their engines. When the lights turn green, it is the signal to go. Timing is all important. If a driver leaps off before the green light, a red light flashes on at the bottom of the pole and that driver is out of the race.

The spectators hear a piercing howl from the two engines as they blast away from the starting line. This is followed by the loud screech of tires trying to get a good grip on the pavement. The dragsters flash by in a blur of color.

Their speed quickly builds up to as high as 240 miles per hour. In seconds they hurtle across the finish line. The drivers release parachutes that spread out behind the cars and help stop them.

It is all over so quickly that electronic timers must be used to decide the outcome. The difference between winner and loser is usually just a few thousandths of a second.

8. BUMPER TO BUMPER AT 175 MPH
Stock Car Racing

During the 1940s a different kind of auto racing was born in the South. It was called stock car racing.

The first stock car races were held in open fields better suited for cows and crops. The drivers were looking for thrills and excitement. Stock car racing was for any young man who was willing to take certain risks—such as taking the family car back home with a crumpled fender or a beat-in top or a burned-out engine.

It wasn't long before some smooth-talking, smart men realized that there was money to be made in stock car

78

racing. There were enough young drivers around to hold car races and charge admission. In place of open fields, they built oval dirt tracks. They put up a first prize of about $20. The only reason they offered prize money was to have an excuse to charge admission. There were always plenty of young men who wanted to race whether or not they won a prize.

"The only reason we're charging is to pay the purse," the promoters said. "And we know you folks don't want to see your favorite driver go home without any money in his pocket!"

The cars bumped and skidded all over the track. The drivers fought hard to win. They went into curves at full speed and slid through almost sideways, spraying the stands with red dirt. Even though it was against the rules, they rammed other cars from behind hoping to cut their tires.

While the drivers were busy racing, the smooth-talking promoters often sneaked away with all of the admission money. Sometimes an angry driver would get in his car and chase the promoter down the road to try to collect his prize money.

Fans loved the sport not only for the thrills, but also because the cars were just like their own. People who drove Hudsons rooted for Hudsons. Other car owners rooted for Chevrolets, Fords, and Plymouths.

In 1947 a man named Bill France and some of his friends formed an association called NASCAR. NASCAR stood for the National Association for Stock Car Auto Racing. Bill France wanted to bring some order to the wild sport that was beginning to have a bad name in the South.

NASCAR made sure the winning drivers got their prizes. They made rules about the making and driving of stock cars. They planned a series of big stock car races.

Today stock car racing is big business. NASCAR holds more than 30 races each year. Most of the races are held on paved superspeedways in the South. The great majority of drivers also come from the South.

The cars still look like ordinary factory models, but in fact they are not. Engines, bodies, and brakes are completely rebuilt to make the cars faster and stronger. Standard tires are replaced by special wide tires which give a much better grip on the road. The doors are welded shut for safety. A driver gets into his car by crawling through the window. He sits in a special high-backed racing seat surrounded by a cage of steel bars that protects him in case the car rolls over or crashes.

Driving a stock car is fairly simple.

The driver just shifts into high gear and goes. The curves are so steeply banked that he does not have to shift down to get around them. The race becomes a test of how fast a man is willing to go around a curve and of how long he can keep going.

The 30 or more cars that enter each race drive bumper to bumper around the track. The race course looks like a crowded expressway during rush hour. The only difference is that the cars are moving at speeds up to 175 miles per hour.

Stock car fans will always remember stock car racer Richard Petty. He grew up in a tiny town in North Carolina. His father, Lee Petty, was a champion stock car driver in the dirt track days of the 1950s. In thirteen years of driving, Lee Petty won 54 races. Few people thought this record would ever be broken.

They're off! The pack gets the green flag at the Daytona 400 (top); Bobby Allison (left) takes the first turn at Trenton; Richard Petty wins the big one at Darlington (bottom left); and the Gregg-Haywood team takes the checkered flag at Daytona.

When Richard was a boy, he spent most of his time tinkering with racing engines and learning how cars work. When he turned 21 he became a driver himself. During the 1960s he broke almost every record on the book—including his father's record of 54 victories. He became known as the King of Stock Car Drivers.

For a long time there was one major stock car race that neither Richard nor his father had been able to win. It was the famous Southern 500 held each year at Darlington, South Carolina.

In 1967 Richard had his best year ever. When he came to Darlington he felt sure he could win.

At a signal the 30 drivers in the race started their engines. The cars went around the track two times to build up speed. When the flag went down, the drivers stamped on their gas pedals. The race was on. Richard Petty led the pack from the beginning. He went into the first curve at a speed of 135 miles per hour. His tires were so hot they were smoking.

He drove so fast that his tires could barely grip the road. He was close to being out of control, but he never let up for the entire 500 miles. When there were only four laps to go, the crowd could see a big smile on his face.

When Richard climbed out of his car to accept the winner's trophy, he was limping. He had taped his thick leather boots before the race. But heat from the exhaust pipe under the floor had burned one of his feet.

Richard was too happy to worry about the pain.

"It took eighteen years for the Pettys to win the biggest one of them all," he told reporters. "But it was worth it."

9. BUILT TO A FORMULA
Sports Car Racing

At the same time that stock car racing was getting its start in the South, a lot of Americans began to buy foreign sports cars. People who owned the new foreign cars wanted to try them out in the kinds of races for which they were best suited.

An organization called the Sports Car Club of America, or SCCA for short, was formed in California to put on road races in which amateur drivers could compete. These were called sports car races.

Phil Hill was one of the first American drivers to become interested in sports car racing. Phil got his start as a midget car driver. Midget cars were small, inexpensive autos that ran on short, oval dirt tracks. But Phil also owned a sleek, expensive new Jaguar, and he was eager to try it out. He wanted to enter one of the road races held on the winding roads along the rugged California coast.

Phil drove in his first sports car race in Santa Ana, California. At first he tried to drive his Jaguar the way he did on dirt tracks. He headed into the first sharp turn at top speed. He found out quickly that road racing is very different from driving on a banked oval track. He spun out on the turn and ran into one of the bales of hay that lined the course. When he got back on the road, he drove with more control. He finished the race in second place.

Phil went on to become the best sports car driver in America. He and a few other American sports car drivers began to compete in the world's biggest sports car series, Grand Prix racing.

In 1958, when Phil Hill first entered Grand Prix competition, Grand Prix races were being held all over the world. Each year a Grand Prix event took place in Monaco, Holland, Belgium, France, England, Germany, Canada, Italy, South Africa, Mexico, Argentina, Morocco, and Portugal. In each of these contests, the world's best drivers raced in the world's most advanced sports cars. These were built to a "formula" especially for Grand Prix racing and were called Formula 1 cars.

The drivers won points for placing in each race. At the end of the series of races, the driver who had won the most points was named the World Champion Driver.

By the end of the 1961 Grand Prix series, Phil Hill had almost enough points to win the title of World Champion Driver. For most of his life, he had dreamed of being the first American to be named the best driver in the world.

As more and more American drivers began to enter international road races, promoters decided it was time for Grand Prix races to be held in the United States. The first U.S. Grand Prix race took place in 1961 at Watkins Glen, New York. The 2.3-mile course dips and swings in sharp curves over the lovely countryside of the Finger Lakes region of upstate New York. A second U.S. Grand Prix race is now held at Ontario, California.

In 1966 the United States and Canada began a big, professional sports car series of their own. The series of six races was sponsored by the SCCA and the Canadian Auto Sport Club. It was called the Canadian-American Challenge Cup, or Can-Am.

Can-Am racers: John Surtees, first Can-Am champion, in his Lola-Chevrolet; Mark Donohue, 1973 winner, in his Porsche + Audi; Warren Agor, 1974 entrant, in a McLaren-Chevrolet.

Each race in the series was 200 miles long. Four of the races were held in the United States and two in Canada on courses especially made for professional sports car racing. They were designed to provide the challenge of driving at high speeds over winding country roads.

The first Can-Am series was a huge success. Over $300,000 in prize money was up for grabs. Top drivers and cars were entered. Drivers came from international road racing, Indianapolis racing, and American sports car racing.

A former World Champion Driver, an Englishman named John Surtees, was the first Can-Am champion. A close second was Mark Donohue, a great American driver. Both drove English-built Lola cars powered by highly improved Chevrolet V8 engines.

The Can-Am cars are pure, streamlined racing machines. They are larger than the

Formula 1 Grand Prix cars because they are required to have two seats and full bodies like amateur sports cars. The usual combination is an English body, such as a Lola, powered by the American V8 engine. Some American car bodies are also used. The Can-Am racing cars are as fast as any road racing cars in the world.

The first weekend of October, the time of the Grand Prix event, Watkins Glen, New York, is in a party mood. The town is host to world-famous racing car drivers and thousands of visitors. From many parts of the United States and Canada, countless spectators gather at the start-finish line. Other groups watch from hilltops along the circuit.

At major auto racing events, spectators do not watch just the main contest. They also thrill to the qualifying runs which take place before the big contest.

The cars line up for the race according to their qualifying speeds. The drivers are in their seats. Nothing but the tops of their helmets and goggles can be seen.

Officials hold their stopwatches ready. The green flag flashes. The racers roll quickly down the first stretch of the course. In seconds the drivers have their machines at high speed. The roar of the engines is ear-splitting. It is difficult to identify drivers as they speed along at more than 200 miles per hour. Favorites can be followed only by spotting the large numbers on the bodies of the cars.

Lap after lap the slim, speedy cars blast along the straightaways and up and down hills. Booming into the curves, the drivers shift gears and brake a little to slow down. As the cars slip around the turns, the drivers try hard to keep them from sliding out of control. At the curves the sharp odor of scorched rubber is the strongest. Large groups of people gather at these points to watch these amazing machines in action.

Today's superfast race cars look more like flying missiles than automobiles. They are designed almost as scientifically as a rocketship built to go to the moon.

Car designers use computers to plan streamlined body shapes. The designs are tested in wind tunnels so that scientists can see which body shapes move fastest and most easily through a stream of air.

The cars are so low to the ground that the tires stick up higher than the bodies. The contestants drive almost lying down.

These streamlined race cars go so fast that they need something to keep them from flying. Upside-down wings are added to hold the cars to the ground.

Designers make the cars as safe as they can. They know that the safer a car is, the faster it can be driven. Many

94

Spectators jammed the stands to see the start of the 1974 Grand Prix contest at Watkins Glen.

safety devices that are first tested and proven on racing cars are later used on passenger cars that are sold to the public. Improvements in tires, brakes, steering, and springs, as well as the invention of seat belts and shoulder harnesses, have all come out of the sport of auto racing.

If the Count de Dion could stand at a curve at Watkins Glen and watch the space age cars rocket past, he would stare in amazement. He would find it hard to believe that so many changes could take place in less than a hundred years.

The cars will keep changing. The bold drivers of today will be replaced by daring new drivers. As long as the challenging and hazardous sport of auto racing in all of its many forms offers color, thrills, and excitement, it will continue to have millions of enthusiastic fans.